Mom En Pointe:

A Mompreneur's Guide to

Balancing it All

LaShawn Robinson Yates

Acknowledgements

This book is dedicated to Samira, Landyn, Dakota, and Autumn—the four notes in the music of my life.

This book is also dedicated to any birth mother, bonus mother, godmother, grandmother, adopted mother, auntie mother, community mother, spiritual mother, or matriarch with a dream in her heart.

About the Author

LaShawn Robinson Yates is a mom to four children, ranging from ages 7 to 22. She has been an entrepreneur for over thirteen years with businesses ranging from body scrub, reselling, and jewelry, to podcasting, screen-printing, and photography.

The call to help other mothers in her community came around 2015, when LaShawn started a movement called Work Free Moms. Soon after, she began motivational speaking under the name The Momivator, and later formed a business under the name The Small Business Doula.

In early 2024, LaShawn founded She Did Business, LLC–a rebrand of her existing business The Small

Business Doula. She Did Business is a reference to the Proverbs 31 woman of the Bible, who effectively conducted her affairs at home *and* did business in the marketplace with grace and much success, to the glory of God.

In addition to her active role as a minister of the Word of God, LaShawn is a speaker and serves as a faith-based coach, offering services to visionary mothers and entrepreneurs that struggle with procrastination, self-sabotage, and other mindset issues.

Introduction

En Pointe: a dancer standing or moving gracefully entirely on the tips of their toes.

Mom En Pointe: a mom gracefully taking care of home while tending to her business or ministry matters—even as life keeps her on her toes.

I am so glad you decided to pick up this book. As you read on, I promise to tell you the truth, the whole truth, and nothing but the truth about this bigger-than-life challenge we are called to! Being a "Mom en Pointe" isn't for the weak. It's for superhuman beings. Yep, real life superheroes. That's who we are!

We all should be wearing capes under our blouses and blazers, or hoodies and robes. Seriously! As for me, I always knew that being my own boss was non-negotiable. Even as a young person working at a fast-food restaurant or at the mall in retail stores, I was always more interested in the upper management's role than my own. What was the district manager doing right now? Who is the founder or CEO of this company? What's the backstory? Even in my earliest positions, these were the questions I was asking.

Fast forward to the beginning of my motherhood, (single motherhood at that), when I was working at a manufacturing plant for an international brand in Suffolk, Virginia. I was about twenty-two years old, and only a couple of years out of college. My manager had convinced me to follow her from one company to a new one, where she was the head of the QA department. Someone (I'll call him Joe) changed my life by investing in me. It took me several years before I understood what his kind act really meant.

I was good at my work, bold, outspoken, and carefree. Joe worked in the purchasing department and took notice of my leadership and curiosity. One day, he privately blessed me with a few tiny books and some CDs. I am proud to still have one of the books, *The Treasury of Quotes* by Jim Rohn, on my bookshelf.

I began thumbing through these miniature books that were no bigger than my hand while listening to the CDs (yep, this was back when they were still a thing). It was then that I started to learn the principles of business and integrity. I did not implement all the recommendations at that time, but I had my first introduction to the world of business done the right way (God's way), and I was hooked. I played those CDs on repeat in my car daily and held on to them until they were all scratched up and unusable. It was that foundation, coupled with working for less than I was worth, that created my powerful desire to pursue entrepreneurship.

Whatever *your* reason for choosing entrepreneurship, welcome to the sisterhood! In this book, we will get up close and personal with the elephant in the room. Here, we are going to call a spade a spade. No one wants to talk about just how difficult this journey can be. However, you can choose to magnify the beauty and reward over the hardship and keep your joy while doing so.

I hope that while you read this, you'll hear the beautiful truth—that you are not the only one who struggles, and you are not the only one who is *tired* (some days that's 'tied' and if you know, you know). You are not the only one with your sight set higher than anyone around you might understand. You are not the only one working toward a legacy for your family, and yet finds herself last to be served. If you can relate, you are not alone.

- LaShawn

Chapter One

Make it Ok

Any given day, along the way…

"*I'm hungry, mommy!*"

The half-sleep and barely audible, yet politely whispered demands were all too familiar to me. My brain starts screaming frantically "no, no, nooooo!" Wait—this was the morning I was going to practice ten minutes of mindfulness, I reminded myself. Ten minutes of prayer, stretching, self-care, or whatever. I was finally going to wash my face and brush my teeth *before* I catered to the kids! I *promised* myself—ugh! And yet, my precious children stand at the side of my bed with crust in their eyes and dried drool stains beckoning me to my motherly duties.

"*Mommy, I'm hungry. I want cereal and 'shocket' milk.*" says one. (Here is where I want to say come back when you can say the word 'chocolate' properly).

"*I want Lucky Charms!*" says the other.

"*I want oatmeal!*" says the last.

By this time, it's like a full-blown chorus. To be honest, when I started this motherhood journey, I didn't even know that incoherent little ones with drool stains and eye crust could bust out a full menu of demands at six o'clock in the morning. The possibility just never crossed my mind! However, I soon discovered that they absolutely *can*. So, there I lay with just one eye open, hair all over my head because the bonnet can't even act right, and I'm dog tired, annoyed, and humored all at the same time. Have you ever been there? I mean, where is a personal chef and nanny when you really need one?

Next comes the hard part; but only if you allow it to be hard. You put your feet on the floor after wrestling mentally with your current reality: the unfairness of being pulled on from sunup to sundown, the truth that you have *once again* lost on the priority scale, and the (occasional) sadness of the day's monotony which lies before you. Yet, tired and begrudged, you step into your ballet slippers and begin to tie them up. Deep breaths. Your stage awaits. It's time to dance. There are moments when this dance can hurt, my friend. Particularly when there's a dream inside of you that hasn't seen the light of day. It might be a business waiting to be born. It might be an unanswered calling on your life. The result can look like extreme discomfort, mental pain, and anguish—all from bearing the weight of motherly duties while a nagging desire is left unfulfilled.

After entering the kitchen one day with what felt like my 49th request of an edible or drinkable thing by one of my kids—only to be called on by another kid with a completely different need (ugh!)—I hit my kitchen island at full motherly speed, completely pivoted on one foot to an opposite counter, and it struck me: I spin in circles for my children throughout the day. I dance. I am quite literally *en pointe*. Delivering this, changing that, preparing this, driving there, nursing this, sympathizing with that, paying for this, peacemaking here, teaching that, playing with those, correcting there, etc.

Eventually, I had a running joke with my family and friends that I feel like one of those tiny ballerinas you would find inside a musical jewelry box, twirling in a circle of repetition while filling the needs of my family. I coined the term, Mom en Pointe, to illustrate the way that us mothers are sometimes made to feel.

But what about the needs of the world waiting for my personal contribution? What about what I had to offer *outside* the walls of my home? What about my identity as a visionary businesswoman or in my call to ministry, apart from my family? Now before I offend anyone with those questions, please let me make myself clear: The true mompreneur knows she has been called, and whether the calling is in the ministry or the marketplace; she knows it. She just knows. It's as if the calling was imprinted into her DNA. Make no mistake—God Himself put it there!

Does this sound like you? Be honest here. If so, go ahead and get ok with that (*for real*—just stop reading right here and take a few breaths until you feel ok with that). Give yourself permission to want to heed the calling. This road has no room for the condemnation of mom guilt. Here's where we throw that out the window. After all, the greatest success book ever written, the Holy Bible, speaks about a woman of virtue whose behavior is worthy to be modeled. In the book of Proverbs, the thirty-first chapter, we can read about that priceless woman "...seeks wool, and flax, and works willingly with her hands. She considers a field, and buys it: with the fruit of her hands she plants a vineyard. She makes fine linen, and sells it; and delivers girdles to the merchant."

Come ON, woman of God! That screams Mompreneur to me! What does she get in return for all that you ask? Well, the Bible goes on to say that "Her children rise up, and call her blessed; her husband also, and he praises her." This is a mompreneur who has given herself permission to take care of her home *and* take care of her business. Her profit is more than money. It is the reward of praise, admiration, and recognition from her family. What could be better than that?

So, here's where you can let go of the guilt. You can be praised, admired, and recognized by your family for breathing life into your own dreams. Your business.

Your calling. If you have been sitting idly by, waiting for your turn because you had a different perception, it's ok. The good news is, it's not too late for you! So, you too, are a Mom en Pointe. You must do Mom things. Your life consists primarily of "momming". Sometimes just for part of the day, and sometimes for most of the day, with little to no break. Reality check! That's the life God gave you. Most of the time, it is the life that you chose. Make it ok with you. In addition, you're either a current or aspiring business mom. Make that ok with you, too.

But first, you must learn the art of deep breathing (make sure you take that breath in from your toenails, my sister) to avoid throwing an adult tantrum in front of your children that are just doing their jobs by acting like children. My best advice to you for now is to accept the undone. Tomorrow is not as ideal as today, but it sure beats never. If the family's need comes first at any given moment, attend to it.

En Pointe quote:

"You can put your business on the back burner—just don't take it off the stove."

-Your good sis, LaShawn

En Pointe Practices:

As soon as you begin feeling overwhelmed, STOP what you're doing and take a break, no matter what it is (of course, we won't leave the baby in the bathtub). Try one of these instead:

- Pop in your earbuds or air pods and play a song or two. You can ask Alexa to do it for you if that's easier. We all have that song that brings us peace, makes us smile or gets us feeling strong again. That's the one we want here. Put it on and *blast* it. Repeat it a few times if you need to—until the relief comes. That relief could be tears, worship, joy, a refreshed smile, anxiety diminishing, or a new sense of wellbeing. All are welcome.

- Lie on your back on the floor—*yes, on the floor*. If you need an exercise mat or blanket, go for it. Stare at the ceiling. Clear your mind and feel the firm support of the floor as you release the weight. Let gravity take over and try your best to silence your thoughts. Do this for about 3 minutes. The point is to let the weight and tension go.

- Allow yourself to cry. Sometimes, tears must flow. Newsflash! *Crying comes with the territory of "standing on business"!* When you are done, collect and speak life to yourself (a favorite verse of scripture, an affirmation, or an inspirational quote).

- When you begin feeling frustrated or angry, slow down. Be slow, yet intentional, about your actions. When you are tightly wound with stress or a recovering control freak like me, this is contrary to how your body wants to respond because of your increased adrenaline, but it works. I find that I make most of my avoidable mistakes and get most of my personal injuries (like dropping food or stubbing my toe—my *absolute favorite) when* I'm moving too fast while frustrated or angry.

- Choose to show love to one of the children contributing to your negative mood, *despite your feelings*. It really works! This act will replace the negative emotions with positivity. When the warm feelings come back to you, welcome those in. Some of us subliminally hold on to

- our negativity (like a child that wants to laugh, but "isn't ready yet"). It's ok to own your relief and move on.

Chapter Two

Make it Right

I was a college student and a single parent living in Fayetteville, North Carolina when I was introduced to a multi-level marketing opportunity with a famous cosmetics and skincare company. I became pregnant during my sophomore year, and the relationship with her father hadn't worked out. To make ends meet, I worked in multiple stores at the local mall, and was on government assistance.

I lived in income-based housing. My apartment complex was called Staunton Arms. I can remember there was a magnolia flower on the old wooden sign at the entrance. My unit was a tiny, brick corner apartment with one single window AC unit and white plastic clothes lines on the side. Outside the back door, there was a sloping hill that led to the dumpster. I can see it clearly in my mind to this day because one morning I slipped and fell down that hill while pregnant! It was another instance of moving too fast, but I was fine. My beginnings were very humble—when I went into labor, I didn't even own a bed. I was sleeping on a twin-sized air mattress supported by two lidded storage bins (yep, the standard issue purple Walmart kind).

At that time, I didn't wear makeup or lipstick but that didn't matter to me. I was desperate to make a better life for me and my only daughter. When I heard of the opportunity, I immediately saw dollar signs. The fancy marketing materials gave me all the feels. After attending a few of those supercharged meetings, I really believed that I could change someone's whole life with those products. Even better, this company was a household name. It truly was a no-brainer for me.

You. Couldn't. Tell. Me. Anything (insert clapping emojis). My recruiter had invited me to an event in Raleigh, NC to hear a top-earning sales executive speak. The energy in the hotel conference room that evening was at a megawatt level. There was chatter everywhere, and brightly colored dresses and sequined blazers in all manners of pink, black, and white. Evidently, the lady we'd come to see was a big deal. Her first name was Gloria. I saw people lined up with their backs against the walls, and those in the back of the room near the doors were pressed together like sardines in a can trying to get an unobstructed view. I wondered what this woman had to offer that was in such high demand.

When she hit that stage, I quickly understood the hype! She had a fierce short haircut, elegant poise, larger-than-life confidence, a huge winning smile, the whitest teeth, and a sharp suit. There were sparkly pins all over her jacket indicating her status within the company. She was eloquent and educated, genuine, and unrehearsed. And please do not get me started on those jewels! She wore big, chunky, 'I'm rich' kind of jewelry. To top it all off, she was a woman of color, which really resonated with me because prior to that, I hadn't seen many examples of wealthy women of color in the flesh.

That woman worked the place like a true professional, sharing her story of success and igniting every heart in the room. She sure stole mine! Best of all, she came down off the stage and as the planets aligned, she walked down the side aisle and stopped at my seat. My heart nearly leapt out of my chest when she put her hand on my chair. I smiled with excitement. Then while still talking, she sat down on my lap—my lap—throwing her head back as she gracefully kicked out one stockinged leg with her stiletto-heeled toes pointed to emphasize her point. Now I couldn't tell you what she was saying at all because I almost passed out. All I knew was that my lap had been blessed by the best! I just knew she had rolled up to the event in a pink car and I was determined that I had next. It was on. That was my magic moment, or so I thought. The razzle-dazzle had me in a chokehold. I felt like I'd been inducted into a special sisterhood or something! I just *knew* she had picked up on my inner sales mojo I mean, she must have seen that "halo" around me, right? . Nope! I was just a prop during a talk.The "signs" were all in my head.

Did I ever mention that I am a natural introvert (strike one)? I cringed at the cosmetic company's promotion of "small talk". Actually, I used to avoid people at all costs (strike two). I really didn't want to approach a woman and ask her to betray her favorite lipstick, all because mine was better. I didn't even like to wear lipstick. I felt like a little girl trying on mommy's makeup! I just hadn't yet acquired the wisdom to care about enriching someone else's self-esteem—I was still trying to find my own (strike three).

When all was said and done, it really was a no-brainer, because my brain was nowhere around when I decided to join that company. They say that hindsight is 20/20 and looking back, I realize that my heart was never in it. I was being fueled by my desperation for more money and I had been sold on someone else's dreams and convictions. Because of that, I found myself out of several hundred dollars from placing a "top level" order.

I volunteered to do makeup for proms, weddings, and events to gain sales and earn some of my lost cash back. But it didn't end there. I wasted time, because while I was great at applying makeup, I didn't like to talk to people, I was extremely uncomfortable with approaching strangers and taking an assumptive sales approach. And the lists of people closest to me that I was supposed to be calling? The sheer thought of it made my skin crawl. Nope. I was not gon' be able to do it. The truth is, that *my story did not match the mission* so I flopped. It was a terrific opportunity—just not the right one for me.

Since that time, I have recovered from a lengthy list of flops. As a mompreneur with a bigger repertoire of failures than successes, I know what it is like to be jack of all trades, yet a master of none. I've been a fast food worker, a retail employee, a waitress, a shoe salesperson, a lab technician, a jewelry-maker, a supervisor, a manager, an inspector, a pest control person, a t-shirt line founder, podcaster, a team member with multilevel marketing in both the cosmetics and wellness industries, a body scrub maker, a homemaker (the hardest job on earth), a reseller, a commercial loan processor, a custom prayer accessory maker, a teacher, a secretary, a project manager, and a banker. I sucked at many of those. I have thrived in the comfort of secure employment, felt the sting of being laid off, carried the crushing weight of being unemployed, and enjoyed the freedom of self-employment.

I've come from being a single Business Mom of one child to a married Business Mom of four children and have since overcome a devastating divorce. Oh yeah, I have had utilities shut off and cars repossessed. Did I leave anything out? I promise you that whatever your circumstances, you can overcome them and find success!

In fact, you must do it. You owe it not only to yourself to make God's business for you *your business,* but you owe it to your children. The bible reminds us that, "A good man leaves an inheritance for his children's children" (Proverbs 13:22). No pressure, right? Seriously though—I encourage you to examine your pursuit. Over the years I have found that when you are headed in the right direction, you will feel that thing in your bones. So, what is it that you have utter conviction about? What are you an expert in? What real-life problem can you help solve? What does your local market need? What has life woven in the fiber of your being that you must share with the world? I guarantee you that if the subject of your business pursuits comes as naturally to you as your blood flows through your veins, you won't ever have to look far for inspiration.

Let me add that you don't have to have a formal education, either. You don't need a certificate, some costly credentials, or a letter of recommendation when you know that you know the space that you are supposed to be in (granted, there are some industries that require certification but as a general rule, you and what you hold inside of you are enough). If you work outside the home, ask yourself if you are supposed to be in that space, doing that job. It might be God's plan for you to seek promotion. Maybe you were meant to run the company!

You can't be afraid of change. If money is what prevents you from considering change, let me encourage you: you will be more enthusiastic once you start to head in the right direction. Enthusiasm results in effectiveness. Effectiveness translates to better revenue for you. Can't you just see the positive reviews, promotions, word-of-mouth referrals, testimonials, and boost in income that will come from a more enthusiastic and effective you?

You can't afford to sit down on your vision. What good will it do you to stand at the edge of a cliff with your wings spread and never take the leap? Just picture that. We spend so much time "almost" being ready. At some point, you have to develop enough nerve to jump! Otherwise, all you'll be left with at the end of your life is the most amazing story of your *intentions*. Sit with that for a moment. When your time is winding down, do you want to share stories of your great *intentions*, or would you rather have been a *doer* of those intentions and lived a great life? The choice is yours. What I know is that most of us do not want to leave a could've/should've life legacy. It doesn't matter if you are the brand, or you represent someone else's. Whether your business involves hair, makeup, jewelry, skincare, essential oils, legal care, insurance, finance, real estate, coaching, speaking, service, or your own creation, what matters is that you are in the right space for you.

The thing is, you can't 'stay in your lane' if you don't know which lane you should be driving in. Rest assured that your life, to this very day, has given you all that you need to start this journey and stay the course. You have a unique "business fingerprint", formed by your natural talents and life circumstances. You will have to look within to mine your own knowledge and excavate the treasure that you can use to generate income—but I promise it's in there.

En Pointe quote:

"Your path has been carved. You just have to get out of the woods to see it."

-Your good sis, LaShawn

En Pointe Practices:

Take inventory of your life. Go deep and ask yourself these questions about your current business:

- Does your current business help, heal, or offer hope?
- If the business itself does not, are you able to "turn" the business model in a way that it can?
- Are you still excited to wake up each day and work on your business?
- Has God spoken to your heart about another direction, and you are battling fear with that change? Be honest with yourself. If you feel that you have been driving in the wrong lane professionally, it's ok! U-turns aren't always easy, but God makes no mistakes--this is your time! You cannot believe the voice in your head that says that it is too late for you to flourish.

Reinvention looks good on us! There is nothing more attractive than a woman who is aware and confident in her purpose here on Earth. Finding your lane will ignite a permanent flame that no one will be able to put out. Don't worry if you find yourself swimming in uncharted waters—God is an awesome life preserver.

Chapter Three

Make it Real

Now that you have embraced your truth and done some reflecting, you should know if you are in the right business lane. If you have decided that where you are currently is where you are supposed to be, congratulations! If you've decided that a U-turn is in order, congratulations again! Either way, you are on the right track. Now, let's talk about keeping it real.

We all know that no two people share the same fingerprints. Even twins, having shared the same womb, have different fingerprints. We are each uniquely made. You may notice that if you watch the most successful people, they tend to be comfortable in their own skin. They embrace themselves wholeheartedly and refuse to let others define them. Just look at Genesis 1:26—And God said, "Let us make man in our image, in our likeness, so that they may rule over the fish in the sea and the birds in the sky, over the livestock and all the wild animals, and over all the creatures that move along the ground." (NIV)

Now consider Psalm 139:14 which reads, "I praise you because I am fearfully and wonderfully made; your works are wonderful, I know that full well." God fashioned you with His hands, with His image as a template. Think about that. Also, if we are fearfully and wonderfully made, as the psalmist indicated, we must be something special. When was the last time you took notice of something fearful and wonderful that didn't stand out? I beg you to *not* fit in.

I need you to be accepting of that lisp you have, or that quirky laugh you possess. You must grow to be ok with being totally random and occasionally blurting something out from left field. You need to know that it is your delivery, your creative presentation, and the way you are wired that will gain your genuine followers and loyal customers. Honestly, they will love you—*if* you aren't afraid to show the world who you are. Are you giving the world the chance to love you, or are you offering up a mask? Deep down inside are you asking them to love a diluted version of their favorite influencer (simply because you are inspired by that person), or are you giving them the full-strength you? Are you selling recycled, watered-down gas-station coffee or a freshly brewed cup? Which would you prefer? I'm just going to sip my tea and leave that there (pun intended).

Here is where the work comes in. I am going to ask you to find a mirror and take a good look at yourself. Yep, find one right now. I'm serious about this. Do not read any further until you do. I guarantee you that I will find out if you skip this step! Get your mirror, sis! Stand or sit in front of one or grab a compact mirror. Next, you are going to look at yourself. Directly in the eyes. Mmhmm. This may be uncomfortable at first, because we don't spend enough time in that place of honesty. Dwell there. Take yourself in. That's right, you need to become comfortable and learn to love all of yourself.

This includes the features you've always tried to hide, your awkward posture, your current weight, the clarity of your complexion, your features, the way you walk, or your voice. These are the things that sometimes scare us the most to share with the world, because they make us vulnerable and subjective to others' opinions. However, these are the things that will make you memorable, and that people will come to love.

Here's a transparent moment for you—I can be awkward, and my jokes are corny sometimes; my features are uneven, I've hated my nose in the past, and I also just discovered that I have a wandering eye. When I'm really inspired and in thought while recording a video, my eye just low-key walks off on its own! Remember that people will have their opinions whether you are mediocre, or you choose to soar! You need a mind shift—consider your unique characteristics as your bread and butter instead of viewing them as hindrances. You might become "the lady with the _____"! But at least they will be talking about you and your brand! That beats zero recognition and zero sales any day, sis.

Reality sells and acting does not. Most potential customers will be able to tell if you are being genuine or not. Look beyond your immediate circle of friends, family, and acquaintances—if they haven't made you rich by now, those people are not going to contribute to your prosperity. Get good with that! It means that as you grow your circle larger, you will eventually connect with people that accept—and find value—in you. For now, until you come to terms with who you are, the people who need you most (those you will serve) will be left without you. Please don't leave them waiting for too long!

En Pointe Practices:

Practice makes comfortable (that's right, it makes comfortable—forget the old saying—we weren't created to be perfect). Effort makes for successful practice. Try these:

- Take a day to try on assorted styles of clothing at a department store or thrift store (thrift stores are my favorite) so that you can learn which cuts, colors, and fabrics of clothing flatter you most. Purchase what makes you feel like the winner you are. If you must tug on, stretch, adjust or second guess an item, then it doesn't come home with you.

- Make videos of yourself consistently and play them back. Get used to the sound of your voice (I don't care, I don't care, I don't care; you must) and critique yourself on the effectiveness of your tone, annunciation, and verbal inflection. Adjust and repeat until you are pleased. Slow down to avoid tripping up on your words. Give yourself grace.

- Get in the mirror and talk to yourself. Affirm yourself with positive talk. Intentionally look yourself in the eyes and tell yourself that you love yourself. Do this often and mean it. This is not for the sake of vanity. This is for the sake of self-love and acceptance where you are right now, whatever it looks like.

- Be gentle with yourself. Remind yourself to stop with the "comparison" games that our minds try to get us to play sometimes. The thoughts will come up, and they are natural. However, you are no one else. There will only ever be one you, so be confident and purposeful when you show up!

The goal is to shift the atmosphere when you enter a room. Make them take notice, but with all humility. Our goal should be to impact your customers while making an impact for the Kingdom of God.

Chapter Four

Make it Now

Pablo Picasso once said, "Only put off until tomorrow what you are willing to die having left undone." We live in an unpredictable world, with a million things to distract us at any given time. Yet, you chose to invest your time in the ministry or the marketplace because you agreed that you were called to do it. If this is true, then you have to answer the call—repeatedly.

Every Mom en Pointe knows how well the bed sheets and comforter *comfort*, and how enticing the TV can be (cue Netflix opening sound). The pillows *pull you in*, and we can 'doom scroll' on our phone for hours. But are any of these things lining your pockets? If one of those is, email me so you can put me on game. Will they help your family in the time of monetary crisis? Do they pay for college tuition? The unfortunate answer is no. You are going to need to become an immediate expert at self-will. There will be times that you will need to do jumping jacks, grab coffee, and wipe tears to get moving or to stay awake.

When you are facing temptation to procrastinate, you must remind yourself that uncommon people have uncommon success because they are willing to do uncommon things. Channel your feelings into gratitude that you have the energy to burn the midnight oil, while others may be sleeping. Ask God for the grace to carry on, and for supernatural refreshing when you do finally get to sleep—even if it is for an hour or two. We are not above all-nighters. They shouldn't be a regular thing, but a Mom en Pointe can dance all night, as well. We are built for this.

My favorite motivational verse when I'm feeling "tired" is Proverbs 24:33-34 which says, "A little sleep, a little slumber, a little folding of the hands to rest—and poverty will come on you like a thief and scarcity like an armed man." I know those are some strong words; but don't they change your perspective? I have met that thief. I know the feeling of being robbed by poverty and "held up" by scarcity.

I can think back to the times when I didn't have a couch in my apartment and only had those fold-up lawn chairs available for guests (yes sis, the basket weave kind people used to watch the fireworks with). Or times when I had the familiar hot flash of embarrassment creep up from my neck to my ears as when I saw the total of my grocery bill, only to have to ask the cashier to start removing items from my purchase so that I could pay for it. There is nothing like having to park several lots over in your apartment complex to avoid a car repossession or whisper while you prepay inside the gas station because you only have less than five dollars (all of which I have done). I have endured many years of scarcity, so the possibility—notice I didn't say guarantee—but even just the *possibility* of a better life has forced me into motion.

Can I challenge you further with a revelation that God gave me? What if I told you that there is a hole in the economy of your home, your church, and your community all while you are trying to determine if your timing is right? Have you ever watched someone play double-dutch and the conditions are perfect for the person to jump in, but they just keep rocking back and forth? So irritating. What about being stuck in traffic in a line of cars and the lead car refuses to turn, even when it is crystal clear for them to go? How frustrating is it being a spectator waiting for them to get in the game?

I imagine that is how God sees us, when we unfairly excuse our fear and lack of faith as being patient or waiting for the right time. The right time will never come knocking on our doors. It is our responsibility to seize the moment, use what we have, and watch the time *become* right. There are vacations not being planned, memories not being made, savings not being stored, responsibilities not being met, irreplaceable moments not being experienced, and blessings not being given when a Mom en Pointe is not working to produce fruit.

You have been called to a life of entrepreneurial motherhood or you probably would not be reading this book. That said, your family is waiting for the financial breakthrough that is within your hands. Have you not grown tired of the bondage of debt? The worry of how you will get through the month? The terror of needing a hefty sum of money and not having it available to do things like repair a vehicle, fund a child's field trip, or celebrate an upcoming birthday properly? How long will you agree to living and not yet live?

Have you heard of the term "cognitive dissonance"? These two words changed my life. I was starting to feel like one of those misunderstood Renaissance composers or artists—just plum crazy about the vision within my heart that wasn't coming to pass. I was tired of people telling me that it was ok when I knew better. No, it was not ok, and I was freed when I finally heard those words and their explanation. The definition is simply "the mental discomfort or psychological stress experienced by a person whose beliefs do not match up with their behaviors". This phenomenon comes up very easily when trying to care for children while running a business.

You see yourself catching up on administrative

work, networking, sending emails, and the kids see lunchtime, playtime, or movie time. You think you can watch some educational videos online to enhance your skill set, and your baby wakes up from a nap as soon as you sit down. I can recall feeling a sense of anguish at times while sitting on the couch being lazy instead of working—or scrolling on social media, knowing I needed to be working on my business. I even had well-meaning family members try to give me passes for doing nothing! The same ones that, at times, were concerned about my financial wellbeing. How ironic is that? The urge is to look at the enablers of this self-sabotaging behavior as thoughvit is their fault that you are not productive. The truth is, it is no one's fault but your own. Your peace will come when you stop justifying and excusing complacency.

En Pointe Practices:

You'll need to be extremely creative, so work when free time presents itself. Get going every time you get 5 minutes. Fill the gaps of your home life with business opportunities. Guess what? Your time is now. Remember that we are on assignment from God to pursue the business endeavors that He has placed in our hearts. Try these:

- Ignore the criticism and stay out of the company of people that try to make you feel guilty for starting today. If God didn't intend to back you up with the grace and energy to balance home and business life, He wouldn't be pouring into you and causing your heart to desire the manifestation of the thing(s) you are dreaming of right now.

- Set small, clear, and realistic goals every day. I can't tell you how many times I set my mind to work on something, but because I was focused on everything I hadn't completed, I made my goal too big and was discouraged. Ninety-nine percent of the time, none of it got done. For example, if you are a writer, set a goal of finishing a couple of pages or a chapter on a given day—not the whole book. If you want to deep clean a certain room of your house, make it your day's goal to finish one section only. Go top to bottom (separating donations, discarding items not needed, dusting, cleaning, and reorganizing the entire section) rather than finishing the whole room in a day. Setting these micro goals will also give you a sense of pride and fulfillment upon completion.

- Remember to STOP when you have reached each goal and celebrate appropriately. Even if you have the energy to go on, you owe yourself a victory lap. Over time, you will train yourself to want to get started, to finish the goal, and enjoy the celebration. I promise, it's a lovely cycle. You deserve to be celebrated, and don't cut it short unless you have no choice.

- Memorize a scripture that speaks directly to the promises that you are expecting (Jeremiah 29:11 is a classic, "For I know the plans I have for you…"). You can also try reflecting on a scripture that reminds you of what you are *trying to avoid* (as in Proverbs 24:33-34 that I mentioned earlier). Let this be your motivation when you need to press on but are feeling a little weary.

- Know that it is normal to get weary and overwhelmed. Every mompreneur, everywhere, feels this way. Sometimes for days at a time. Repeat the previous step.
- Remember that cognitive dissonance is the name for the mental discomfort you will experience if your actions or lifestyle are not lining up with your vision and beliefs for yourself. If you believe you are a successful entrepreneur, your behaviors must align with that to get out of the cycle of discomfort. If the two are not matching up, welcome that discomfort and let it be the steam that powers your engine to get going again. The goal is that the two will line up and produce harmony, good fruit, and ease in our lives.

Chapter Five

Make it Less

My sister Ashley is thirteen years younger than me. She is on top of the trends and shares them with me whenever she believes they can help. She lives in Oakland, California and enjoys the eclectic metropolitan life—when I began writing this book, I lived in a small town in North Carolina. Ashley didn't yet have any children, so you can imagine how I lived vicariously through her adventures! I consider and try most of her suggestions (except veganism—I have one foot over there, though). One of the lifestyle changes she introduced that resonated and stuck with me was minimalism. Minimalism was not a new concept, but I did have a psychological block come up when she first mentioned it. I mean, we had a family of six at the time! I wondered how on Earth could it even be done?

I decided to try minimalism and took the reins after being frustrated day in and day out with the chore of cleaning through and around all our clutter. We had a lot! All the little clothing for the little bodies (some of which no longer fit), old toys, books that the kids had grown out of, Christmas decorations that would never be displayed again, insignificant items kept in memory boxes from *my* childhood, extra dishes, etc. I started to wonder why I was trying to keep the pans that weren't exactly my favorites, or the extra lids to storage containers that I no longer had. When I looked at what I had been holding on to, it was ridiculous. So, I went in at full force.

In 2016, I was the largest I had been in my entire life. This was after giving birth to my youngest child. I was between a woman's size sixteen to eighteen immediately afterwards and for far too long beyond her birth. For context, I wore a size two after my firstborn was born. I had endured several miscarriages, and my hormones were all out of order (there were nine losses in total, the last being a twin pregnancy).

Now this conversation is not about the number on the scale, and I recognize age was a factor in my life too—but so was depression, anxiety, and unhealthy, emotional eating. I used to love me some baked goods and sweets when life got hard! They just didn't love me back! I also realize that we are all built differently. In the Black community, there is a lot of talk about being "big boned". My response to that was always that my bones did not grow when I put on extra weight. Judging by the daily aches and pains, I think my bones just got angry with me, if I am being honest.

So after I left Delulu Land (that's right, the Land of Delusion)—I went through and donated my dream clothing stash. You know, the stash of clothes that I would 'one day' be able to fit again, only in my dreams. I told myself that by the time I reached a healthy size for my body, I would afford myself a new wardrobe. And that was that. After what seemed like countless boxes, bags, and trips to the local Goodwill—I was freed of the extra weight that had been following us from house to house.

    I began to see countertops and shelf space again. I no longer had to touch things that had no function for us to clean beneath and around them. I was able to locate certain clothing items with ease because I didn't have to browse through options that weren't really options. Now, this is a frequent practice in my home because I recognize the freedom of having less to look at and go through. I can't recommend it enough—especially for moms of multiples.

This concept can be used in your business too! I'll use myself as an example: I'm a hippie at heart, a scientist, an artist, and a true creative. I'm a daydreamer—right-brained and messy at times (although it is organized chaos; I can find the remote under the stack of paperwork, in the corner of the shelf in the back). That is my true nature. I love big words, and appreciate detailed explanations of how things work. I'm imaginative, yet logical. If you aren't tired just reading all of that, I'm impressed. What I'm saying is that I can be all over the place and do the most. Yet, I thank God for adaptation! In business, one of my biggest lessons was that my customer is not me! Most of them are not interested in the "fluff" that we tend to think is necessary and makes things "pretty" or acceptable. The only thing trying to do the most will do is tire you out.

We only have a limited time to make an impact.

Your customer can be left feeling lost and turned off if you leave them to get through the weeds because your message isn't straight to the point. What exactly am I saying? If your brand message is edgy, then don't try to make it sound like Mother Goose. If it is lighthearted, spare the heavy storyline. If you are selling empowerment, the sob story has to end somewhere! Does this make sense?

Just like I had to look through my closets and cabinets, you'll need to evaluate your business marketing frequently to see where you can trim the fat. Only use what is useful. That will result in less to manage, less to print, leaner content, and less effort for your customers to get to the juice. The juice is what they came for! If you take too long to deliver, they will leave thirsty and go to another store; believe me, I have learned from experience.

En Pointe Practices:

Don't be afraid of the term "minimalism". It is your friend and can be invited into your home and business little by little. Think of minimalism as a guest in your home. You can give it the guest room—it doesn't need to kick you out of your master suite. Start in the area that has been untouched for the longest. This may be inside of a garage, a kitchen cabinet, a closet, or an office. Try these:

- Resist the resistance—stay focused on the long-term benefits. I donated every VHS movie we owned, along with a little black VCR/TV combo. My ex-husband loved animation and put up the biggest fight (I know, you thought I was going to say the children, right?) Neither of them talked about the TV or the VHS tapes after the night they went away. I promise your family will *not* overthrow you; they will be thankful for the stress-free and tidy environment though.

- Do yourself a favor: envision your future for a moment. Isn't success on your radar? I'm referring to the kind of success that makes a no
- ticeable difference in your life. If your answer is yes (and it should be), then what will that skirt or that suit that doesn't make you feel drop-dead gorgeous mean to you in a year? In 5 years? Will you be able to afford the best for yourself? Of course you will. Let it go. The small oil stain, the linty pill balls on your fabric, the shrunken or twisted appearance, the falling hem, the missing button, the worn thighs, the fading, the discoloration, the nostalgia, and ill fit—can all afford to go.

- Remember there will always be more—more gifts, more purchases, etc. It is fine to entertain these new additions to your home. Minimalism is about living while evaluating what is important. Find what works for you. Don't throw the baby out with the bathwater.

Chapter Six

Make it Last

As I write this chapter, I cannot help but think back on a conversation I had with a sister-friend of mine one day. We had a very transparent talk about our reluctance to network with others (I was very closed off in the past), and the distinct reasons why we were hesitant. It turns out that I was just an introvert and did not see the necessity of follow-up. It just would not register with me. It was like I had done the "hard part" just showing up and "people-ing" so when the event was over and I could breathe again (joking), I could not muster up the strength (and had no desire) to reach back out. When I became active in the church, I attended various conferences and meetings where I had the opportunity to talk to, embrace, swap business cards, and connect on social media with some extraordinary people.

There were countless opportunities for connections that might have resulted in tremendous blessings and business—both for me, and for them.

It was never that I didn't think we could benefit from growing a relationship. It wasn't even that I thought that the people couldn't help me. The fault was all mine. My executive branch was broken. I had all the ideas, and I could talk the talk. Many times, however, I just didn't finish. Since my normal functioning system was to never finish what I started (I was a serial offender), follow-up was the last thing on my mind. I still remember one woman, and how knowledgeable and full of wisdom she was. She was gentle, well-spoken, articulate, and intelligent. I was so impressed with her and wanted to learn more about her. I never took her up on her offer to meet for lunch. In fact, I never saw her again. I am not sure why she sticks out, as there have been so many missed chances, but she does. I pray all is well in her life, but I will never know.

My sister-friend had an interesting take on this networking issue. Her problem had not been her lack of follow-up so much as a lack of participation from the other party when she *did* reach out. She would call these people she was trying to network with and be met with no answer or return call. I was perplexed by this, and even almost had the nerve to judge those people about their *audacity to not call my friend* back or follow through. I asked myself, "Who do they think they are?" That's when it hit me like a ton of bricks—I realized that those people were just like me (ouch).

Here is the deal: community is the answer to your success. I know that is going to be a tough pill to swallow for those of you that are natural introverts like me. I am telling you what I have come to know for sure.

If it were not so, you would not require a customer or client. The definition of business, according to the Oxford Dictionaries, is "the practice of making one's living by engaging in commerce." This can be further defined as the practice of making one's living by "experiencing" the "activity of buying and selling, especially on a large scale". The key word is exchange. The exchange requires other people. We. Need. People.

Quite frankly, we need people just as much as they need us. What we give to each person may vary, just as how much we accept from others. The fact still stands that there is an exchange. You don't want the first exchange to be the only one that your customer makes. Business shouldn't only consist of talking someone into what you are selling. Your special personality should be what brings them back. You want your customer to feel that "once is not enough". What do you offer that will keep them coming back?

I'll tell you what you have to offer. Your reputation and integrity will keep them coming back. They mean everything. I have had to do my share of apologizing whenever I did not deliver on my promise. I didn't understand just how much that could tarnish a reputation, until I was on the receiving end. Think about it—how many times have you said to yourself, "I can't believe she didn't show up!" or "Oh, now he's not going to pick up the phone?" How many times have you wondered how a person could commit to something and leave you or a loved one hanging? It makes you mad, doesn't it? It leaves a bitter taste, right? So don't be that person. There is nothing wrong with a slice of humble pie every now and then. It is easier to apologize (and mean it) for not showing up when you were supposed to, or even backing out of a commitment, than it is to look a person in the eye after ignoring them or pretending that you did not let them down. You would be crazy after that to think they would want to have a conversation with you, much less support your business going forward.

What do you do when you've messed up? You may have to accept the loss of that relationship or consider having a conversation or writing a letter where you are able to convey your sincere humility and offer a genuine apology. You will also need maturity and grace to accept if they aren't willing to hear you out. Here's the thing: you can protect yourself from having to apologize frequently by using wisdom on what you agree to do and be a part of. When your time is not full of things you feel *obligated* to do, then you will do what you *desire to do* with full attention and with joy.

Keeping in contact with people and being genuinely interested in their lives will result in lasting relationships. Aiming to protect your reputation and operate with integrity at every turn will also result in meaningful and lasting relationships. These habits and character traits will make you a winner in your business and personal lives. Honestly, business and living are just more beautiful when the journey is shared with someone. The people you meet may or may not end up doing business with you, but in the end, you can rest assured that if God sent them, there is purpose. Will you decide to nurture those purposes? Or will you miss them?

En Pointe quote:

"If you value your 'yes', people will respect your 'no'."

-Your good sis, LaShawn

En Pointe Practices:

Community is essential to your success. Pray that God protects your heart as you open it to others. Try these:

- Don't be afraid of people. I realize this is easier said than done. Many times, they are nervous too! If you are an introvert like I used to be, practice at the grocery store. Throw out a compliment while in line to check out. Talk about the weather…literally. Smile and say hello when you lock eyes with another patron at the gas pump. These little acts of putting yourself out there will boost your confidence in dealing with others. I smiled and waved to a stranger one day and she smiled and waved back. I had to celebrate!
- Always treat each meeting as an opportunity to serve. Service to others is the highest honor.
- Practice humility. Speak less and listen more. When you speak, try not to talk mostly about yourself.

- Do not be afraid to open up. Give your number, get a number, or exchange social handles. Call people and return their calls. Respond to their comments. DM them back. If you are having a difficult day, it's ok to wait before you answer so that your tone is pleasant. You'll find that the joy of fellowship has the power to overcome what killed your mood to begin with.

- If you say you are going to do something, do it. If you have committed to breakfast or lunch, clear your schedule and be proactive. If you must cancel, be prepared to explain, and do not wait to hear from the other person to do it! If you are going to be absent, you must reach out!

- Foster connections. If you know someone that can be of assistance to or give somebody's business a boost, be the bridge (with consent of course). You will find so much joy in watching other people soar with your help. You can know that you are sowing good seeds, and that your harvest will be abundant.

- Don't forget that you reap what you sow. When you become the kind of neighbor, business partner, or friend you want to have, you will most often gain those kinds of people right back.
- Remember that loyalty is something you cannot buy.
- Focus on the quality of time spent over the quantity of time.

Chapter Seven

Make it Beautiful

Being a Mom en Pointe isn't fair. It isn't supposed to be. You are answering two (or more) vastly different calls at the same time. Some days you might have to ask yourself if you should do research and development right now or dinner? Post some new content or play at the park? Work on your advertising or wipe that nose? Stay late, or be late? Remember that you are uniquely equipped to do both.

The key to embracing your call is to validate your feelings. Own it. Maybe you feel like it's more than others have to contend with, and you would be correct. It seems unreasonable to have your laptop open next to the stove or sit at soccer practice with your computer on your lap. I have been there. Perhaps you're having a tough time embracing the fear of going live on social media with your *real* life happening in the background. Do your kids look a little rough around the edges? If they do, great! That likely means they have had fun today. You are doing a fantastic job. Are there clothes piled up on the bed? At least you washed them! High five! Do you have dishes in the sink? Cool! That means somebody cooked and your family ate! Way to go, sis!

It took me four kids to learn that making life beautiful means letting go of perfection. There is no other Earthly way to do this thing. You might see the funny meme of the mom or dad saying if no one is bleeding, don't bother me and I would say that while some might find that extreme, it's not far from the kind of mindset you need to adopt. The kids will be fine if their shirt has food on it. You are not neglectful if they get sand in their hair (though it sucks, tremendously). The shoes will get scuffed up! If they spill the juice or water, it'll dry eventually! Free yourself, please.

This might be the hardest lesson to learn. I used to be a very anxious, high-strung, tightly-wound, controlling parent. That was so hard to admit, but so necessary. I want those that deal with these issues to understand that letting go was the best thing I ever did. I would overreact when things were broken or spilled or when small mistakes were made. I was projecting onto my children that the only beautiful way to be, was perfect. We all know this is far from the truth! The beauty is in the *experience*, not the *outcome.*

I remember I let my two middle children put on snow suits in the summer (with no shirts underneath) and stomp and splash and run through a huge mud puddle (at the time we lived on a farm). The puddle was big enough for a grown man to lay in and deep enough to come up to your ankles. I *never, ever, ever* would have done that before that day, and it was such a beautiful memory for us all. Their dad jumped in it, and I did, too! I was huge and pregnant with my youngest, but I still had a fun time! Mud ended up everywhere; it covered our shoes, arms, legs, faces, and in our hair. Those of you that share the same heritage I do know what a sacrifice the hair was (lol). Several years later, the pictures and the stories of that day still cause all our faces to light up with joy.

Lastly, I want to name the most toxic and costly trait a mom can have. I can name it because it used to be part of my story. I'll call it the Motherly Martyr Syndrome. I was the martyr that nobody asked me to be. As a mother, I gave myself away each day, looking for a reward that would never come. I wouldn't delegate anything to my children (robbing them of the opportunity to grow responsible) and I bent over backwards to make sure their needs were met. This included cooking, cleaning, washing dishes, homework assistance, laundry, packing snacks and lunch, selecting outfits, maintaining hair and haircuts, walking the dog, etc. I would tire myself out to the point of exhaustion and then be full of resentment for having nothing left to give to myself. Sis, my piece of advice: don't be like me.

En Pointe quote:

"There is no honor in putting everyone else first and perishing in the process."

-Your good sis, LaShawn

Please do not mistake me. I understand that God blesses, and you are recognized for doing the best job you can as a mother and marketplace/ministry figure. I also know that the Word says in Proverbs 4:7, "Wisdom is the principal thing; therefore get wisdom: And with all thy getting, get understanding." Use wisdom and please learn that you must tend to yourself and *carve out* time to breathe. When I tell you that I used to be so stressed out that I did not even breathe properly, I mean it. I could not tell you how many years of my life I spent shallow breathing. I was already at risk due to severe hypertension—I had developed preeclampsia with all my youngest three children and had to deliver each of them via Cesarean section. My high blood pressure did not ease upon delivery. It hung around. At one point, I was certain that I was going to pass out one day and die. I mean that with every fiber of my being. My testimony is but God!

One day, one of my pastors shared Acts 3:19 with me. It says, "Repent ye therefore, and be converted, that your sins may be blotted out, when the times of refreshing shall come from the presence of the Lord". All I heard was 'times of refreshing'! I was like, yes! That is *exactly* what I need like yesterday! While I understand the scripture refers to a consequence of repentance, I could also interpret it as a consequence of communing with God and leaning on His grace.

So, I began to take small breaks.

I stepped outside and let the kids run around and scream in the house.

I practiced slow, deep, intentional breathing. My lungs and brain *really* needed it.

I did my best to tune out the same kid's show song I had heard for the twenty-third time that day (baby shark, do-do-do-do-do-do).

I practiced regulating my heart rate.

I had a child with some health challenges, so I cried privately when I got a moment.

I stuck my head in the freezer (literally) to get a break and some sensory relief.

I laid on the floor often (see Chapter 1). The kids

were happy to join me and crawl all over me or lay down beside me.

I found a dark room and sat there.

I picked my battles.

I asked a child to help me sweep or wipe down the counter.

I let them scrape their own plates. It did not matter anymore if there were large pieces of food still left on them.

I gave up perfection.

I got over trying to make everyone read my mind by how worn out I looked. Yes, I thought that would work, and often went out into the community looking like a bum. No lie.

I put effort into my appearance—for me—because I had let it slip (see previous sentence).

I gave myself the grace I would give to my bestie. Can you say that you are giving yourself the kind of grace and encouragement you'd give to your sister or best friend? Let that marinate for a minute because oftentimes, it doesn't line up!

I prayed to God.

I praised God.

Most of all, I read His Word, chose to believe His promises, and accepted that He loved me enough to help me through it all.

En Pointe quote:

"In terms of motherhood, *refreshed is best*."

-Your good sis, LaShawn

En Pointe Practices:

- Whatever rest looks like for you, take it. Often.

- If you are surrounded by a supportive family or network of friends, don't be a martyr. Don't let your pride get in the way. Lean heavily into your times of refreshment and rejuvenation.
- Each time of refreshment will end. Don't allow worry to creep in when you must return to the "real world" of motherhood and responsibility. Pray and bind the spirit of anxiety, remembering that God's grace is sufficient for *each and every day.*
- Speak to yourself gently and give yourself grace. Correct the negative self-talk as soon as you think it, or it comes out of your mouth.
- Remember that you are your own bestie. Don't be out here in these streets disrespecting your bestie.

Chapter Eight

Making It

Have you ever been close to giving up or close to failure and you hear someone say, "You've got this! You can make it!" This happens a lot to me in the gym (lol). That support gives you a second wind, doesn't it? When you've got someone cheering in your corner, it can really give you an extra boost. Would you believe me if I told you that it has taken me six years to write this last chapter? Though it hurts to admit it; It has.

Over those six years, I went through a marital separation, experienced the heartbreak of divorce, lost my footing emotionally, had to start over professionally, decided to return to school, reentered the workforce (I had been a stay-at-home mom), and reevaluated what I wanted to give to the world. God has been my cheerleader in the dark depressions of the valleys and on the peaks of the mountaintops. My family tried but could not always hold space for me or understand. Several friends fell off, unable to handle my burden. Honestly, there were many days that I did not *want* to get back up. Can I be real? I wanted to surrender, give up, and really did not care if someone else had to pick up my broken pieces. Giving up sounded like a break, and I needed one badly. So many times along the way, my patience and endurance wore as thin as a loose-leaf piece of paper. Some days and nights, I thought I would cry until I shriveled up like a raisin. Somehow, by the grace of God and power of the Holy Spirit I was made strong by the joy of the Lord, and I did *not*, in fact, start to resemble a shriveled grape. For that I give God praise!

When I look back, I am still amazed that I was able to put one foot in front of the other and put my hand back to the plow. Choosing to settle back into my God-given calling has been one of the most challenging decisions I have ever made. I felt extreme shame because of my divorce, which I viewed as a personal failure. Today, I give glory to God that playing small and staying in the same place I had come from was worse than the fear of making the choice to spread my wings and take flight.

It was Nelson Mandela who said, "I never lose. I either win or learn." How does that quote make you feel? Have you ever considered putting all your perceived "failures" in a mental file cabinet labeled "lessons" instead? How would that shift change your perspective? God never intended for you to carry the shame of your past into your future. He tells you to cast your cares upon Him, for He cares for you.

All of those lessons are tools in your life's

toolbox; the more tools you have, the more qualified you are for your calling. Remember that your testimony is what enables you to lead other men and women of God out of the places that you have come out of. You are equipped with the power to speak with conviction, know what *you* know for sure, and stand on business more determined than ever. Please remember that it is never too late to turn your breaking into a breakthrough.

En Pointe Practices:

Ask yourself the following questions when making decisions about your hopes, dreams, and business endeavors. Write down your answers. You can use old-fashioned pen and paper, or your notes app on a device. Refer to these answers and modify them as time goes on, to keep your perspective aligned and deal with reality rather than fear.

- What is the worst thing that could happen?

- What is the best thing that could happen?
- What is most likely to happen?
- Are you willing to go through the worst to get to the best?

Try to focus on the best and most likely outcomes. Believe God for the best outcomes. Do this every time fear tries to keep you from moving forward.

My Desire For You

I hope these words have been helpful, as they have come from my heart. I pray that you feel less alone. My desire is that you remain inspired more than ever to stay on your path, knowing God is right beside you to help you overcome every adversity and refresh you along the way. My sister in Christ, I cannot wait to see you dance! I pray you take courage and get up on the world stage, giving it all you've got. I'm cheering you on, and the world is waiting for you! In closing, I would like to share my daily prayer with you. Join me and other mothers around the world daily, in praying for yourself, your business, and your home.

The En Pointe Daily Prayer

Create in me a clean heart O Lord and renew in me a right spirit. Yesterday is gone, and today is a new day. This is the day that you, O Lord, have made. I will rejoice and be glad throughout this day. Thank you that it is you who has given me power to obtain wealth, according to Deuteronomy 8:18.

Enlarge my territory O Lord. Bless me indeed O God. I pray for my increase today God. I thank you that I am above and not beneath; the head and not the tail; the lender and not the borrower. Thank you that I do not have to be afraid of men and their outward appearances or actions toward me.

Thank you for covering my household with your hand. Thank you for your Holy protection. Thank you that your favor rests upon me, Father God. I thank you that there is a season for everything, and my time has not passed but my time is now. Thank you for redeeming my time, restoring what the enemy stole, and the canker worm ate. I thank you that as I work, you are filling my storehouses to overflowing.

Thank you for supernatural creativity and direction. I am grateful for the visions and dreams you have given and will give me concerning my business or ministry. Thank you that my approach will be like no other and my work will distinguish itself from the masses—even if I work in a corporate environment.

Thank you for creating me to be peculiar and unique. Holy Spirit, please Guide me to use my uniqueness for my success. I decree and declare that I've been redeemed from the curse of poverty. I decree and declare that I've been redeemed from a lack of wisdom and knowledge. I decree and declare that I am gaining wisdom and understanding.

Let the words of my mouth and the meditation of my heart be acceptable in your sight, God. I long to bring you glory through my business and ministry and be a blessing to my household and the community. I decree and declare that my bills are paid in full, and I will have more than enough. Help me to remember to have an attitude of gratitude and a servant's heart. I decree and declare that I will not stop, slow down, or give up. I am equipped with everything that I need for today. I am on assignment by you, God, and I mean business.

In Jesus's name I pray,

AMEN.

Mom En Pointe

www.ingramcontent.com/pod-product-compliance
Lightning Source LLC
Chambersburg PA
CBHW020452220526
45464CB00002B/959